The Best Book of

Ponies

Jackie Budd

KINGfISHER

NEW YORK

Contents

Author: Jackie Budd
Consultant: Lesley Ward
Senior editor: Sarah Milan
Editor: Camilla Reid
Senior designer: Sarah Goodwin
Designer: Ruth Levy
Cover design: Mike Davis
Production controller: Kelly Johnson
Illustrators: Lindsay Graham,
Kaye Hodges, Christian Hook

KINGFISHER
Larousse Kingfisher Chambers Inc.
95 Madison Avenue
New York, New York 10016

First published in 1999
10 9 8 7 6 5 4 3 2 1

1TR/1298/WKT/MAR(MAR)/128KMA

LIBRARY OF CONGRESS CATALOGING-IN-PUBLICATION DATA
Budd, Jackie.
  The best book of ponies / Jackie Budd.—1st ed.
    p. cm.
  Includes index.
  Summary: Introduces pony-keeping, explaining
breeding, grooming, riding clothes and equipment,
and riding lessons. Includes a glossary.
   1. Ponies—Juvenile literature. 2. Horsemanship—
Juvenile literature. [1. Ponies. 2. Horsemanship.]
I. Title.
SF3'5.B76 1999
636.1'6—dc21 98-40376 CIP AC

ISBN 0-7534-5172-7
Printed in Hong Kong

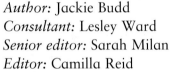

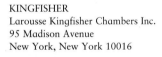

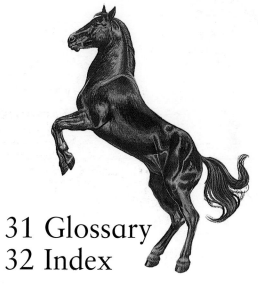

A foal is born

In a grassy paddock on a summer day, a foal nestles close to his mother. Although it is only a few hours since he was born, he is up on his long, wobbly legs. His ears flick to and fro—he is curious about the other ponies in the field and the world around him. In a day or two, he may feel brave enough to join the rest of the foals and take part in the games they play. For now, he feels safer by the mare's side.

Making friends

A little foal has a lot to discover. He will begin to learn all about life with other ponies. By being handled every day, he will soon get used to being around people, too. When he is about four years old, he can be trained to carry a rider on his back.

4

All about ponies

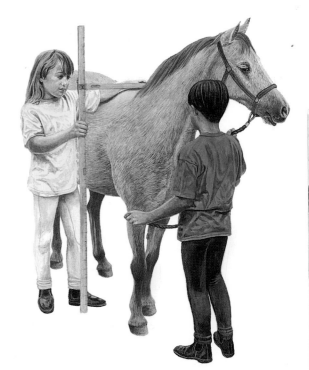

There are many fascinating facts to learn about ponies. Perhaps you have met ponies at a riding school, or you may even have a pony of your own. Discover all you can about them and you will soon become the best of friends.

Colors and markings

There are ponies of many different colors, each with its own name. To tell the difference between them, look at the color of the coat, and of the mane and tail.

Often there are white markings on the face and legs—these have special names, too. Learn these terms so that you can easily describe a particular pony.

How many hands?

All horses are measured in "hands," or units of 4 inches, from the ground to the top of the withers. Ponies measure 14 hands and 2 inches, or less.

Stripe

Snip

Sock

Bay Brown coat with a black mane and tail

Black Black coat and a black mane and tail

Blaze

Stocking

Chestnut Reddish-brown color all over

Palomino Golden coat with a pale mane and tail

The points of a pony

The parts of a pony are called "points." They each have a different name.

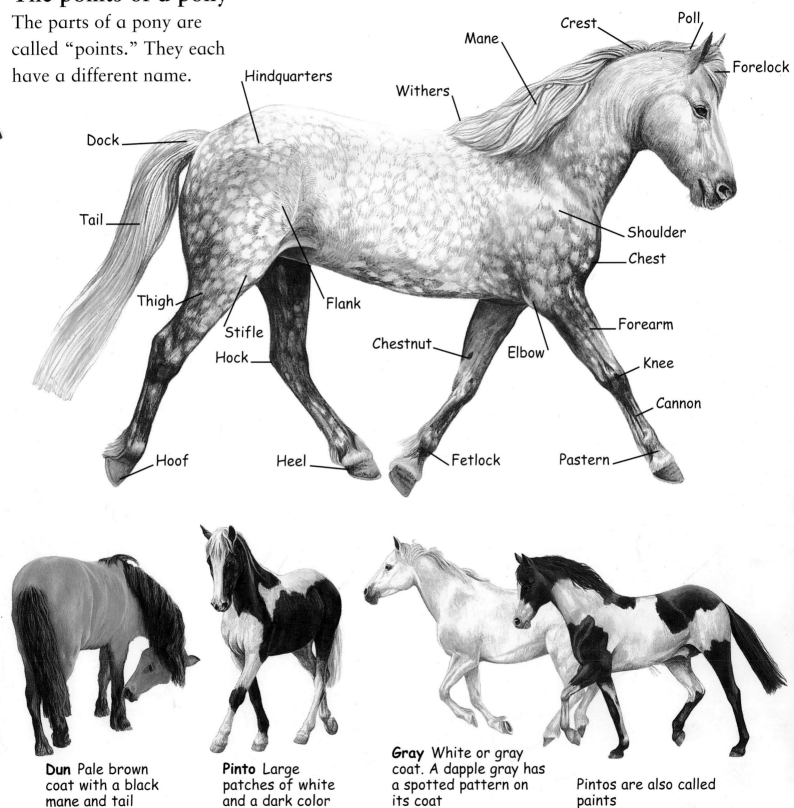

Hindquarters

Dock

Tail

Thigh

Stifle

Hock

Flank

Hoof

Heel

Fetlock

Mane

Withers

Crest

Poll

Forelock

Shoulder

Chest

Forearm

Elbow

Knee

Cannon

Chestnut

Pastern

Dun Pale brown coat with a black mane and tail

Pinto Large patches of white and a dark color

Gray White or gray coat. A dapple gray has a spotted pattern on its coat

Pintos are also called paints

Horses and ponies of the world

Horses and ponies are found all over the world. In each region, breeds have developed to suit the conditions there. And for thousands of years, humans have used these strong, speedy animals to help them in their lives.

Sable Island pony
U.S.A.

Mustang
U.S.A.

Morgan
U.S.A.

Appaloosa
U.S.A.

Quarter horse
U.S.A.

Criollo
Argentina

Falabella miniature horse
Argentina

On the ranch

One of the horse's earliest jobs was to help a rider keep up with a herd on the move. In North and South America, fast and agile horses are still used to help round up cattle.

Fun and games

The invention of machines has meant that there are fewer working horses and ponies around today. We still enjoy training them for sports and other activities. These riders are playing a game of polo.

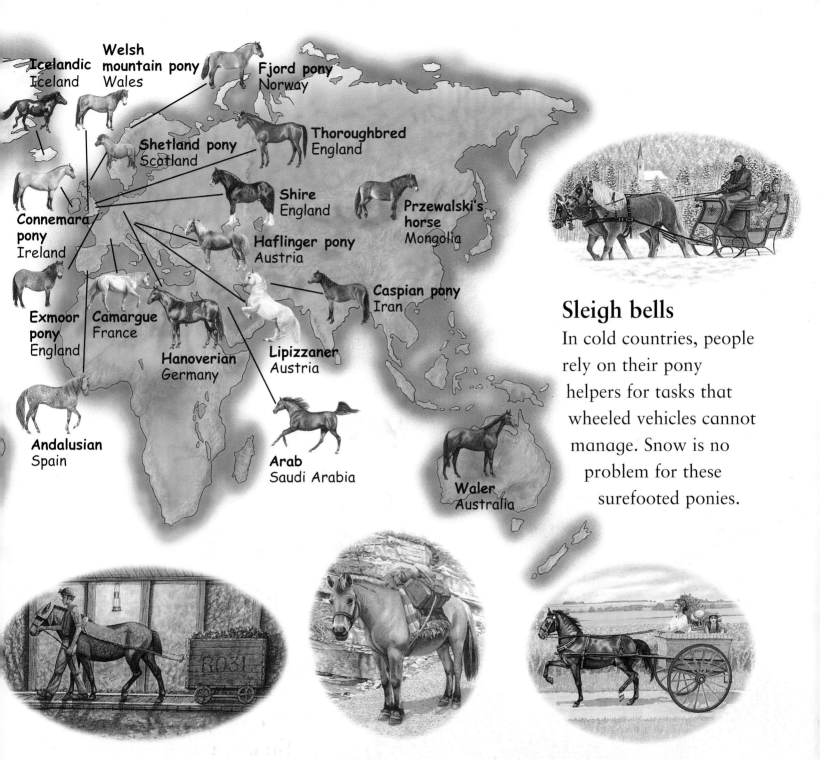

Icelandic
Iceland

Welsh
mountain pony
Wales

Fjord pony
Norway

Thoroughbred
England

Shetland pony
Scotland

Shire
England

Przewalski's
horse
Mongolia

Connemara
pony
Ireland

Haflinger pony
Austria

Caspian pony
Iran

Exmoor
pony
England

Camargue
France

Hanoverian
Germany

Lipizzaner
Austria

Andalusian
Spain

Arab
Saudi Arabia

Waler
Australia

Sleigh bells

In cold countries, people rely on their pony helpers for tasks that wheeled vehicles cannot manage. Snow is no problem for these surefooted ponies.

Down in the mines

Ponies were pulling carts deep down inside coal mines until recent years. It must have been a dark and dirty job, and very hard work.

Packing up

In many mountainous areas, pack ponies are used to carry heavy loads. Survival here would be hard without these sturdy workers.

Getting around

Throughout history, ponies have been harnessed to carts and carriages to carry people and goods over long distances.

9

Ponies of the past

Ponies like these lived in North America thousands of years ago. Sharp eyes for spotting hunters—like this saber-toothed tiger—and fast legs for running away from danger helped them survive. Even so, they died out about 12,000 years ago. Modern American horses are descended from horses brought over by Spanish explorers.

Life in a herd

Ponies love company—staying together in a herd makes them feel safe. In any group of ponies, some will always become special friends. Just like humans, every pony has its own personality. Some may be bossy or grumpy, some are brave and friendly, while others are timid and shy.

Handle with care

Today's ponies still have the natural instincts of their ancestors. They are friendly animals, but even when trained, they can be startled easily. Because of this, it is important to be careful around ponies. Learning about them will give you confidence and help you to win their trust.

Contented

Curious

On the lookout

Stay alert when you are riding. Your pony may see or hear something that frightens him and, as a wild pony would do, he may pull away from it.

Angry

Interested

Making faces

Ponies may feel excited, happy, or angry, just as you do. You can often tell what a pony is thinking or feeling by the look on his face and the way he holds his body.

Catching a pony

1 Whenever you are around ponies try to be relaxed and calm. If you have to catch a pony in a field, walk toward him slowly so that he can see you approaching. Hold the halter down by your side and speak quietly to him.

2 The halter and lead rope are used to lead and tie up a pony. First, place the lead rope around the pony's neck, then reward him with a treat.

3 Avoiding any sudden movements, put the pony's nose through the halter. Lift the strap behind his ears and buckle it up. Praise him and stroke him firmly on the neck.

4 Walk alongside the pony's head, holding the lead rope underneath the pony's chin. Hold the rest of the lead rope in your other hand.

13

The outdoor pony

Ponies enjoy the outdoor life because this is what they would be used to in the wild. In a field, ponies can roam freely with their friends and eat grass, which is their natural food. The field should have strong fencing, fresh water, and shelter. If your pony lives outside, make sure to check on him twice a day.

A coat for all seasons
In the winter, ponies grow a thick coat to protect them from the cold, although ponies with finer fur may need a waterproof blanket to help keep them warm. All year round, there is nothing ponies like more than a roll—it feels good and helps keep the coat healthy.

Stablemates

Some ponies live in stables all year round, while others spend only a few hours a day indoors. A pony's stall must be large and airy so that he is free to move and lie down. Stables should have secure, ratproof rooms in which to keep feed and tack. Tools and equipment should be stored neatly to prevent accidents.

Safety first

It is very important that no one smokes in the stable.

The tack room

Tack is the gear a pony wears for riding, and it is kept in the tack room. Tack should be cleaned after every ride so that it stays supple and safe to use.

Bedding down

The pony's bed should keep the pony warm at night, and be comfortable when he is lying down. There are several types of bedding to choose from.

Wood shavings

Shredded paper

Straw

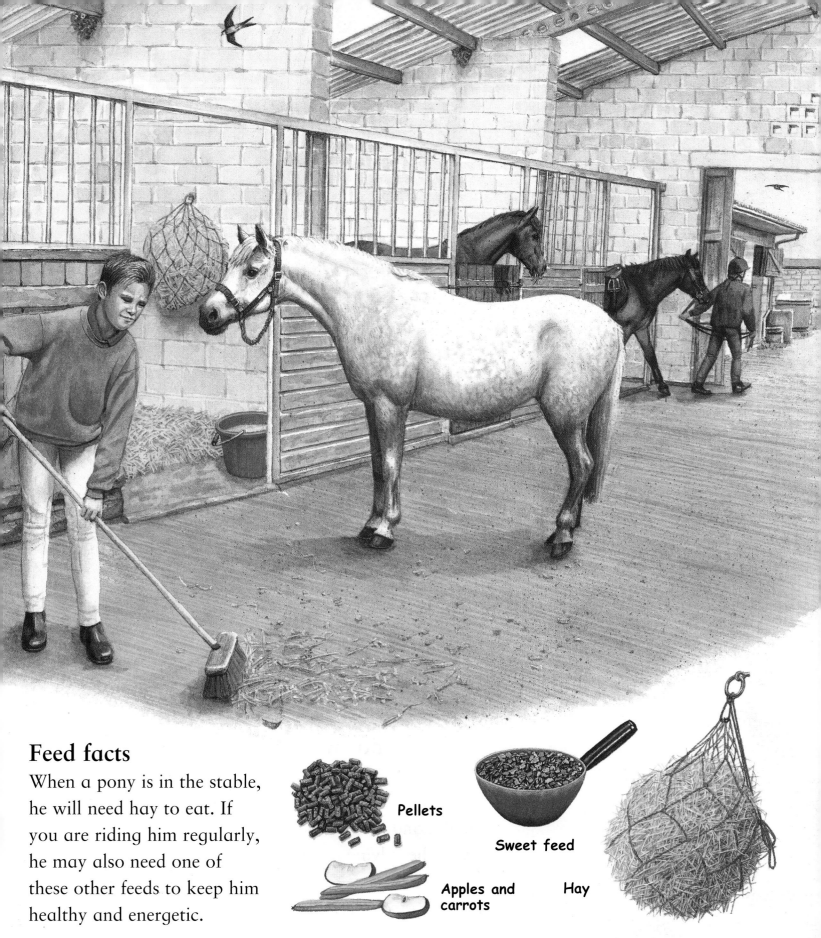

Feed facts

When a pony is in the stable, he will need hay to eat. If you are riding him regularly, he may also need one of these other feeds to keep him healthy and energetic.

Pellets

Sweet feed

Apples and carrots

Hay

Daily tasks

Each day, all year long, there are jobs to do to keep a pony happy and healthy. He needs food and water, and both he and his home should be kept clean and neat. Caring for a pony can be hard work, but it can also be a lot of fun.

Clean and shiny

Grooming keeps the coat glossy and the skin clean. Make sure the pony is tied up, then remove any surface dirt with the dandy brush before working over the coat with the body brush.

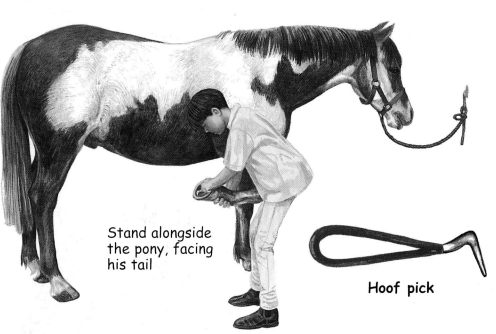

Stand alongside the pony, facing his tail

Hoof pick

Feet first

The hooves should be picked out twice a day. Run your hand down the leg, then ask him to lift his foot by giving the fetlock a tug. Working from heel to toe, remove any mud or bedding.

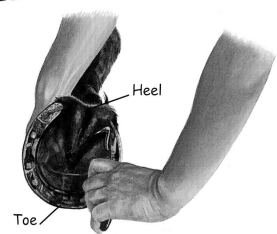

Heel

Toe

18

Dandy brush for removing dried mud and sweat

Rubber currycomb for very muddy or hairy ponies

Body brush for cleaning the coat

Sponge for washing the eyes, nose, and dock

Sweatscraper for wiping off extra water after a bath

Grooming equipment

Grooming a pony is a great way to get to know him. Even if you don't own a pony, you can collect all the brushes and tools you need to look after your favorite riding school pony.

Mucking out

Stalls should be mucked out every day. Lift out the manure and wet bedding with a pitch-fork, and put them into a wheelbarrow. Finally, put in new, dry bedding.

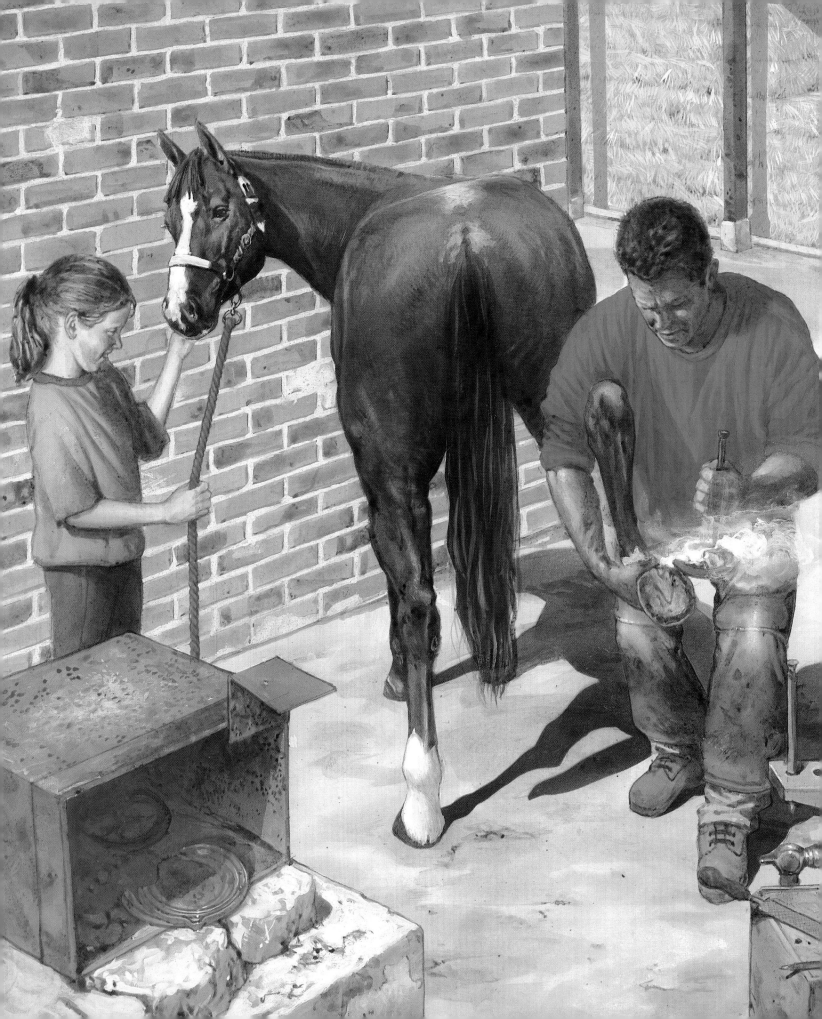

Feeling fit

Bright eyes, a shiny coat, and a lively expression show that a pony is feeling fit and healthy.

To keep him this way, a pony should be well cared for. His feet must be checked regularly by a farrier. If he is ever sick or injured, the vet should be called in to treat him.

New shoes

Without metal horseshoes, a pony that you ride would soon get sore feet. Every few weeks, a farrier should take off the old shoes, trim the hooves, and fit him with a new set of shoes. Just like fingernails, hooves grow all the time, so even ponies that don't wear shoes should have their feet trimmed.

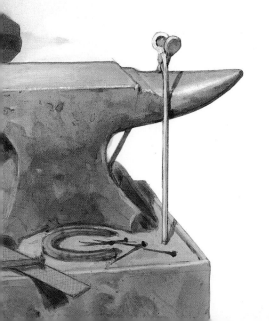

The vet's visit

The vet will treat a pony in an emergency, but vets also help with a pony's routine healthcare. They will check that a pony's teeth are in good condition. They will also vaccinate the pony against disease and give him medicine to keep him from getting parasites such as worms.

Bridles and bits

The bridle is used to control the pony when you are riding him. It is important that the bridle fits properly and is kept clean, so that the pony is comfortable and happy.

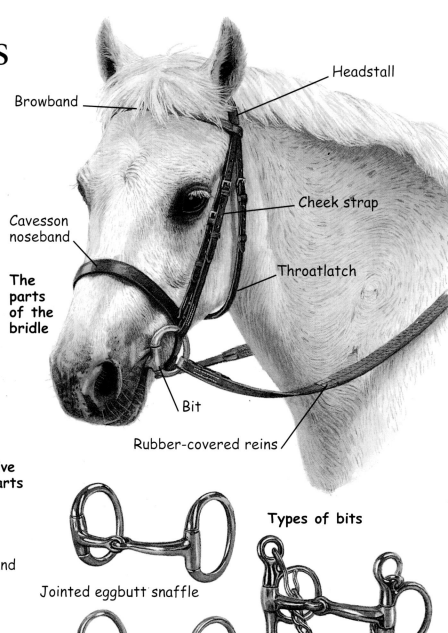

The parts of the bridle

Browband

Headstall

Cheek strap

Throatlatch

Cavesson noseband

Bit

Rubber-covered reins

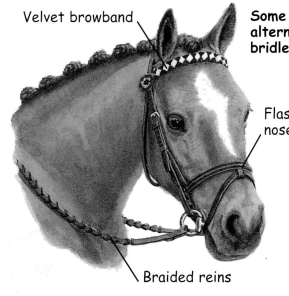

Some alternative bridle parts

Velvet browband

Flash noseband

Braided reins

Jointed eggbutt snaffle

Types of bits

Straight bar rubber snaffle

Jointed Pelham

What is a bridle?
The bridle is a set of leather straps. The different parts can be changed to suit you and your pony's needs.

Choosing a bit
The bit lies over the pony's tongue and is connected to the reins and cheek straps. There are many bits to choose from. Most ponies wear a snaffle, which has a ring at each side and can be jointed or straight. Livelier ponies may need a Pelham.

How to put on a bridle

1 Lift the reins over the pony's head. Hold the bridle in your right hand and slip the bit into the mouth with your left hand.

2 Raise the headstall over the ears, then pull the forelock from under the browband. Check that the bit just wrinkles the mouth.

3 When fastened, you should be able to fit four fingers between the throatlatch and the cheek. Finally, buckle the noseband.

Western riding

Western riding is very popular in the United States and some other parts of the world. For this style of riding, the pony wears a different set of tack. Western bridles have no noseband and are often beautifully decorated. Only a very light touch on the reins is needed.

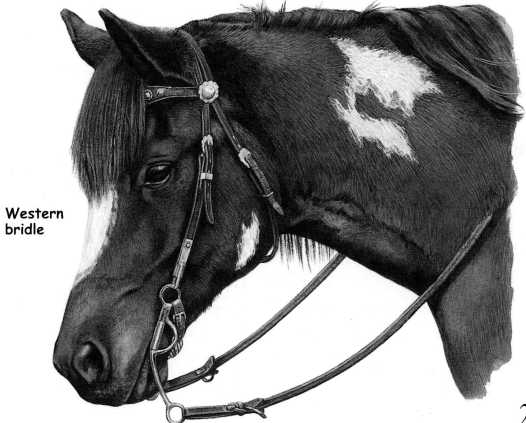

Western bridle

23

Saddling up

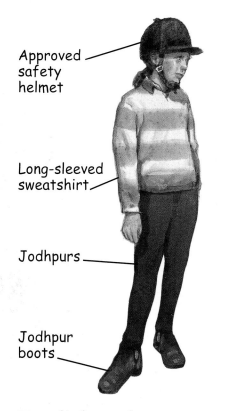

A saddle helps the rider sit securely in the correct position on the pony's back. In this picture, the boy is using a Western saddle and the girl is using an English one. The saddle fastens around the pony's belly by a thick strap called the girth.

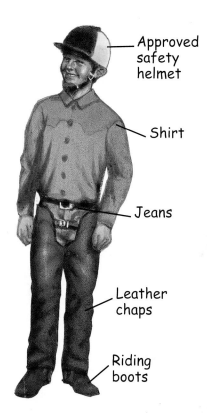

Approved safety helmet

Long-sleeved sweatshirt

Jodhpurs

Jodhpur boots

Approved safety helmet

Shirt

Jeans

Leather chaps

Riding boots

English style
English-style riding clothes are designed to be stylish and safe. Most important are boots with a low heel and a good helmet.

Western style
Western-style riding gear is based on the clothes used by cowboys on the ranch. It is comfortable and very hard-wearing.

Learning to ride

Stirrup iron   Stirrup leather

The best place to learn to ride is at a riding school where instructors can make the lessons safe and fun.

Your instructor will help you choose a pony that is right for you and teach you how to tell the pony what you want him to do.

Stirrup leathers

Check that the stirrup leathers are the correct length by putting your fist on the buckle and the stirrup iron under your arm.

Mounting

Stand on the left side of the pony, facing the tail, with the reins in your left hand. Put your left foot in the stirrup. Hold the back of the saddle and swing your leg over the pony's hindquarters.

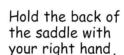

Hold the back of the saddle with your right hand

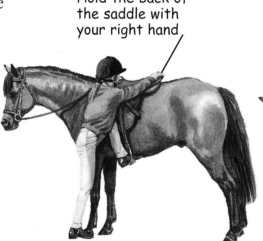

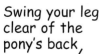

Swing your leg clear of the pony's back

Dismounting

To get off a pony safely, first take both feet out of the stirrups. Lean forward, swing your right leg over the pony's back, and jump to the ground.

Getting started

It is important to sit correctly in the saddle. To ask the pony to go faster, to slow down, or to turn, you will use signals called "aids" or "cues." These are given using your legs, hands, voice, and body weight.

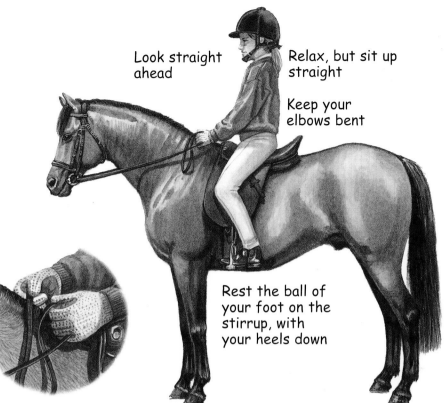

Look straight ahead

Relax, but sit up straight

Keep your elbows bent

Rest the ball of your foot on the stirrup, with your heels down

Hold the reins with your thumbs on top and little fingers underneath

Trot on

A pony has four gaits—walk, trot, canter, and gallop. Trotting is very bumpy until you learn to rise to the trot. This means that you rise up and sit down with his steps.

The canter

As your riding improves, you can try a canter. Ask the pony to speed up by nudging him with your heels. Sit down and enjoy the ride!

27

Going to a show

"And it's a clear round!" There is nothing more exciting than winning a ribbon on your favorite pony. When you get better at riding, you can learn to jump, and even have the chance to enter a show. Jumping takes a lot of practice. Remember to look up, sit quietly in the saddle, and stay balanced over the fence. You and your pony have to be a real team.

On your marks . . .
These riders are taking part in a sack race at a show. Gymkhana events, or mounted games, are like party games on horseback.

From the egg and spoon race to the bending race, all the games are fast, furious—and loads of fun. To be a winner, you'll need both skill and speed.

Pony fun

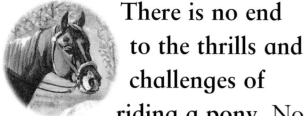 There is no end to the thrills and challenges of riding a pony. No matter what type of riding you choose, there is a whole world of fun waiting for you.

Out and about

Going on a trail ride and exploring the country with a group of friends is always exciting. Together you can ride through woods, across fields, or even head for the hills.

Vaulting

Vaulting is like acrobatics on horseback. Vaulting can help your riding skills, because it teaches you to stay perfectly balanced.

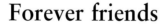

Forever friends

Perhaps you would like to have your own pony, or become a famous rider one day. Maybe you just want to spend time with a four-legged friend. Whatever your pony dream, have fun!

Glossary

aid A signal used by the rider to tell the pony what to do. Aids are also known as cues.

bit The metal part of a bridle that is placed in the pony's mouth.

bridle The headgear that the pony wears for riding.

clear round When you complete a jumping course without making any mistakes, you have done a clear round.

colt A male pony under four years old.

farrier A person trained to fit ponies' shoes.

filly A female pony under four years old.

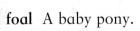

foal A baby pony.

gelding A male pony that cannot father foals.

graze To eat fresh grass.

groom To brush and clean a pony.

gymkhana event Mounted games, or races on horseback.

halter A piece of tack used on the pony's head for catching, leading, and tying up.

hand The unit used to measure a pony's height. It is so called because it is about the width of an adult's hand. Horses are 14 hands and 3 inches, or more, in height. Ponies measure 14 hands and 2 inches, or less.

mare An adult female pony.

mount To get on a pony. Getting off a pony is called dismounting.

near side The left side of the pony (from his point of view).

off side The right side of the pony (from his point of view).

paddock An enclosed grassy area where ponies can feed and exercise.

points The parts of a pony.

reins The straps attached to the bit, which you use for controlling a pony when you ride him.

saddle The piece of equipment used on the pony's back to keep the rider in position.

show An event where ponies and riders can compete in either showing classes, jumping classes, or gymkhana events.

show jumping A jumping class at a show that takes place in an arena, over brightly colored fences.

stallion An adult male pony that can be used for breeding.

stirrup The part of a saddle where you put your feet.

tack All the gear needed to ride a pony, which includes the saddle and bridle.

trail riding To ride your pony in the open country rather than in a ring or other enclosed area.

Index

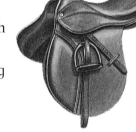